2B

PIANO
Adventures®

...allenging pieces with
changing moods and
changing hand positions

by Nancy and Randall Faber
THE BASIC PIANO METHOD

Production Coordinator: Jon Ophoff
Cover: Terpstra Design, San Francisco
Engraving: Dovetree Productions, Inc.

FABER
PIANO ADVENTURES®

ISBN 978-1-61677-605-3

Table of Contents

("Gold Star" characteristics of each piece)
Color the star gold or put a star sticker for each piece you learn!

Page

Festive Sonatina

1. Allegro

Nancy Faber

FF1601

DISCOVERY

Where does the musical idea for the *coda* appear earlier in the piece? *measure* _____

2. Moderato

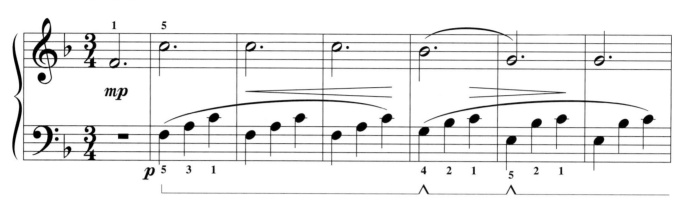

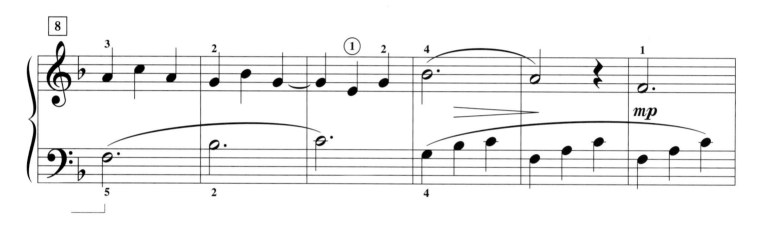

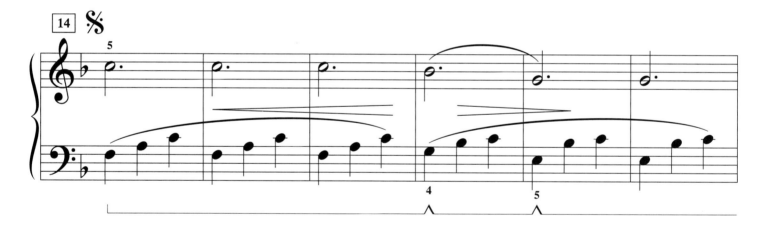

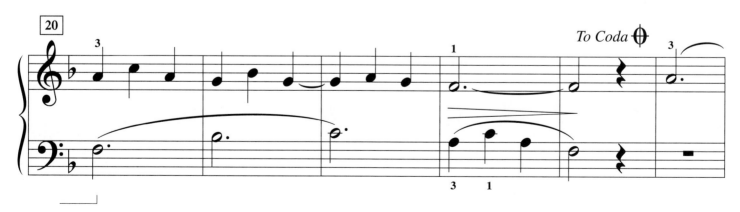

FF1605

DISCOVERY

Transpose *measures 1-25* to **C major** and **G major**.

3. Vivace

DISCOVERY

Label the *form* of this piece: **A B A¹**, (partial return of the A section) and ***coda***.

Tijuana Tambourine

Nancy Faber

Fast, with energy, "in two"

FF1605

DISCOVERY

Transpose *measures 1-16* to **C major**. What interval does the RH use to start? _____

What will be the top note of this interval? _____

Cat Prowl

Words and Music
by Nancy Faber

FF1605

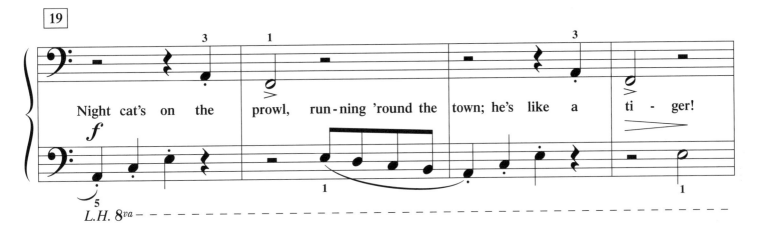

Night cat's on the prowl, run-ning 'round the town; he's like a ti - ger!

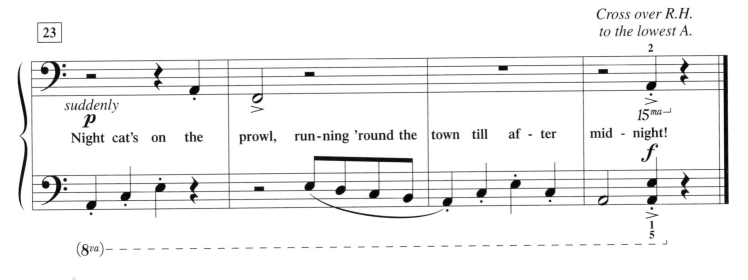

Night cat's on the prowl, run-ning 'round the town till af - ter mid - night!

DISCOVERY

What **minor chord** is formed in the *first* measure?

Aria
(Theme from *La Traviata*)
Libiamo ne' lieti calici

Giuseppe Verdi
(1813–1901)
Arranged by Nancy Faber

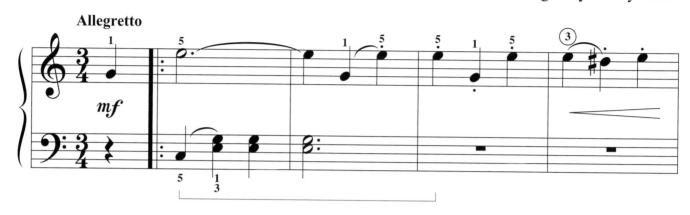

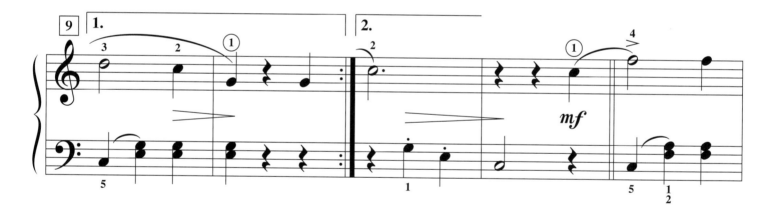

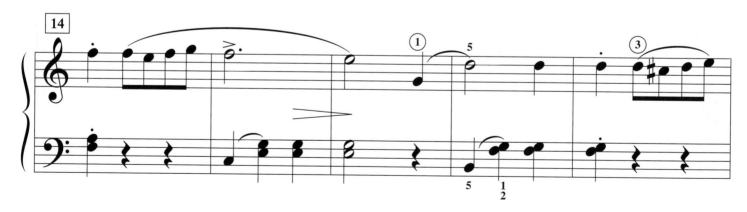

FF1605

DISCOVERY

Label the harmony in each measure as **I**, **IV**, or **V7** for *measures 13–24*.

The Little Tin Soldier
Secondo

J.L. Malloy
Arranged by Nancy Faber

*Suggestion: Circle all the repeat signs in red to quickly catch your eye when playing.

FF1605

The Little Tin Soldier
Primo

J.L. Malloy
Arranged by Nancy Faber

DISCOVERY Is this piece a march or a waltz? Tell your teacher why.
Hint: Think about the **time signature**!

Secondo

FF1605

Primo

*Listen for this rhythm in the *secondo*.

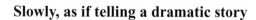
Gypsy Dance by Firelight

Nancy Faber

Slowly, as if telling a dramatic story

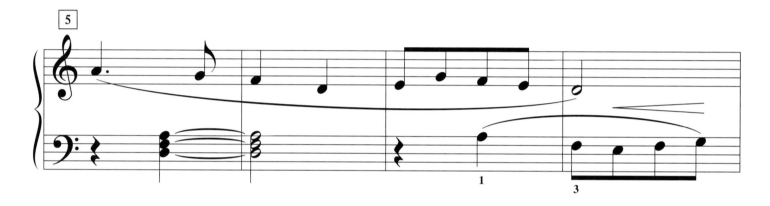

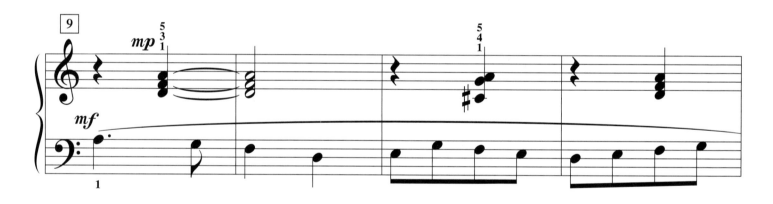

FF1605

Treasure Island

Nancy Faber

With energy

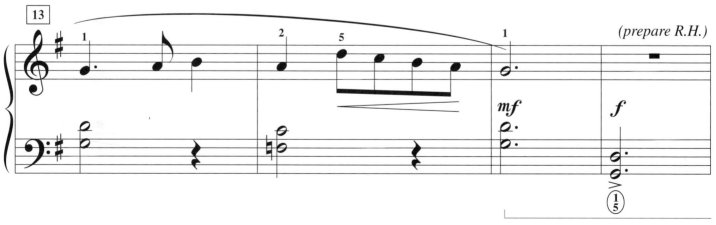

FF1605

DISCOVERY

Why is it necessary to put a **natural** in *measure 3*?

The Phantom Complainer

Words by Jennifer MacLean
Music by Nancy Faber

Moderately, as if telling a story

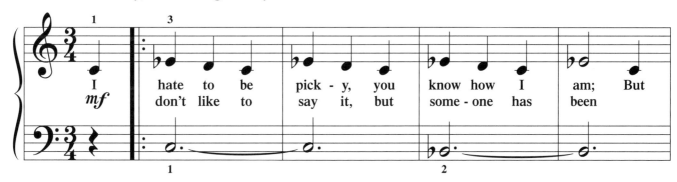

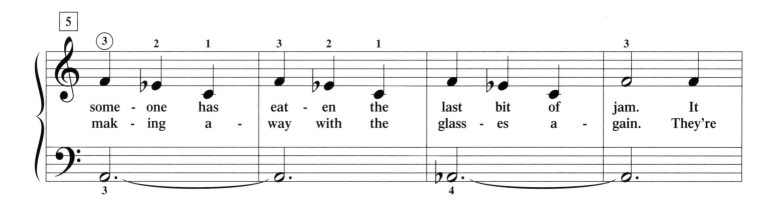

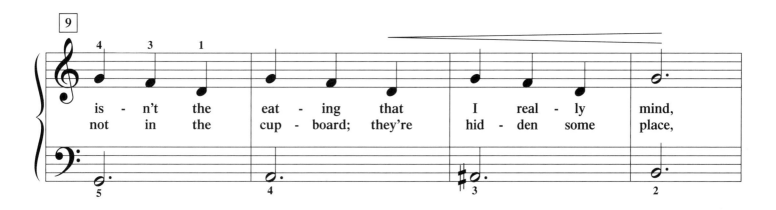

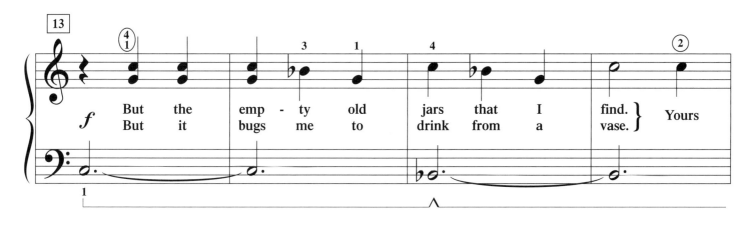

DISCOVERY

Point out a *fermata*. What does it mean to do?

Rainbow Sister

Chinese Folk Melody
Arranged by Nancy Faber

FF160

DISCOVERY

Transpose *measures 1-16* to **G major**.

Banuwa
(Village)

Folk Melody from Liberia
Arranged by Nancy Faber

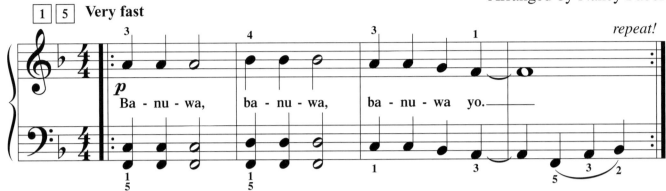

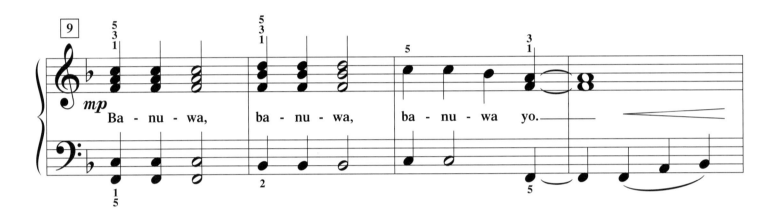

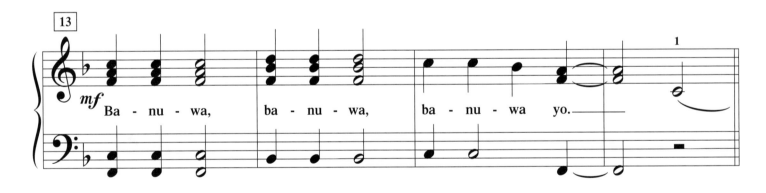

FF160

DISCOVERY

Transpose *measures 1-24* to **G major**.

FF1605

Misty Midnight Garden

Nancy Faber

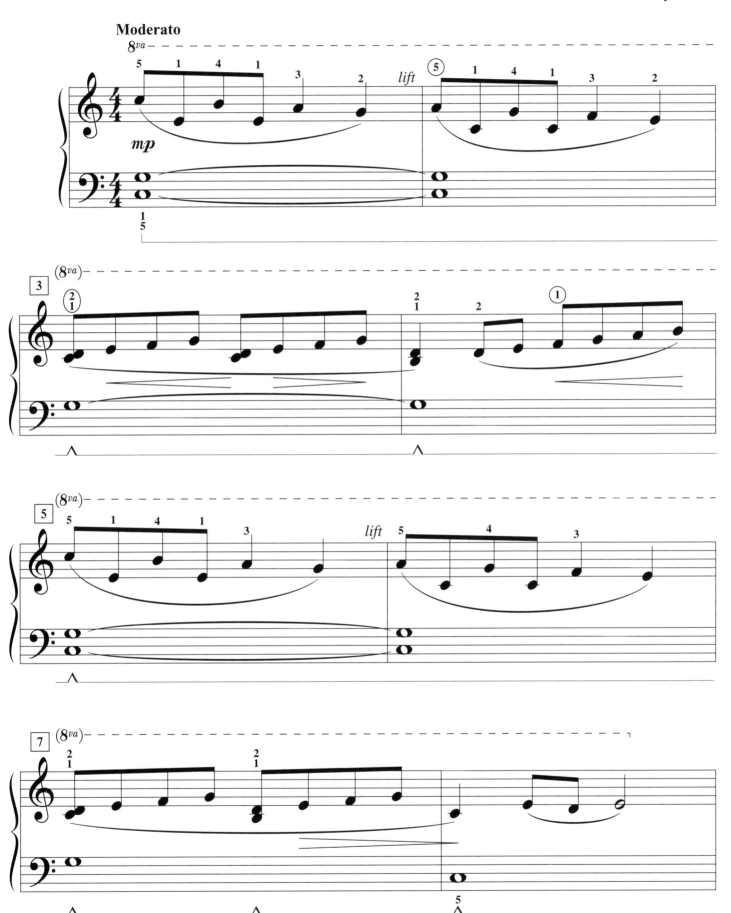

D I S C O V E R Y

Where is there a **time signature** change in this piece? Tell your teacher what it means.

FF1605

37

Gold Star Dictionary

Circle a gold star when you can pronounce each term and tell your teacher what it means!

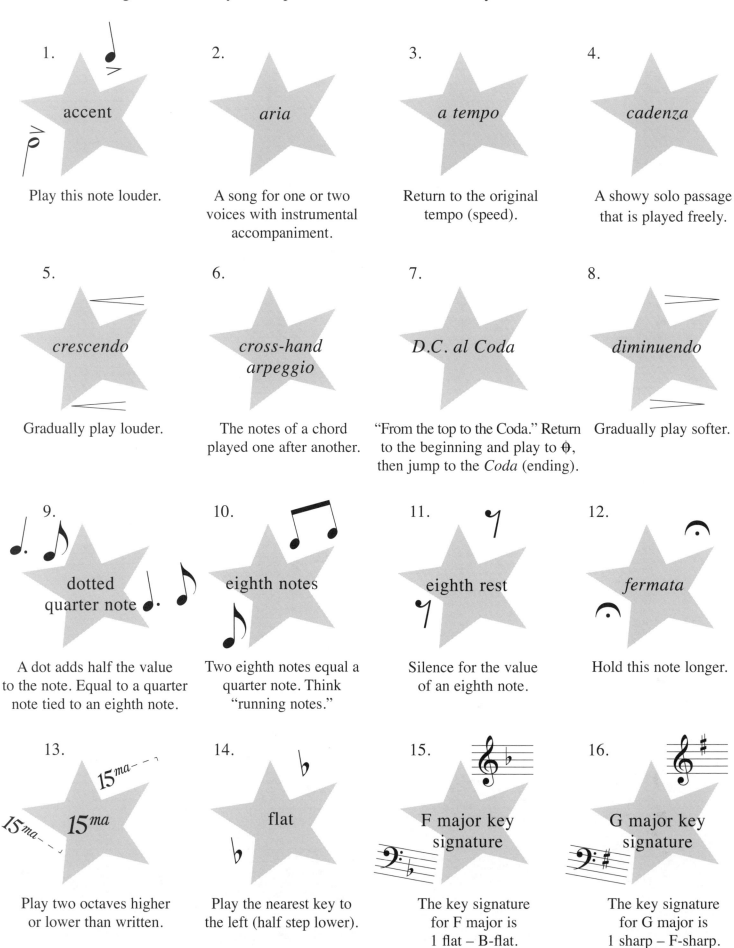

1. **accent**

Play this note louder.

2. *aria*

A song for one or two voices with instrumental accompaniment.

3. *a tempo*

Return to the original tempo (speed).

4. *cadenza*

A showy solo passage that is played freely.

5. *crescendo*

Gradually play louder.

6. *cross-hand arpeggio*

The notes of a chord played one after another.

7. *D.C. al Coda*

"From the top to the Coda." Return to the beginning and play to ⊕, then jump to the *Coda* (ending).

8. *diminuendo*

Gradually play softer.

9. **dotted quarter note**

A dot adds half the value to the note. Equal to a quarter note tied to an eighth note.

10. **eighth notes**

Two eighth notes equal a quarter note. Think "running notes."

11. **eighth rest**

Silence for the value of an eighth note.

12. *fermata*

Hold this note longer.

13. **15ma**

Play two octaves higher or lower than written.

14. **flat**

Play the nearest key to the left (half step lower).

15. **F major key signature**

The key signature for F major is 1 flat – B-flat.

16. **G major key signature**

The key signature for G major is 1 sharp – F-sharp.

FF1605

17. grace note

An ornamental note that is played quickly into the note that follows.

18. forte *f*

The Italian word for loud, strong.

19. ledger line

A short line used to extend the staff.

20. mezzo forte *mf*

The Italian words for moderately loud.

21. mezzo piano *mp*

The Italian words for moderately soft.

22. natural

Cancels a sharp or a flat (always a white key).

23. pedal change

Lift the damper pedal as the note is played. Depress the pedal immediately after.

24. pianissimo *pp*

The Italian word for very soft.

25. piano *p*

The Italian word for soft, gentle.

26. ritardando *rit.* *ritard.*

Gradually slowing down.

27. sharp

Play the nearest key to the right (half step up).

28. slur

Connect the notes over or under a slur.

29. staccato

Play detached, disconnected.

30. time signature $\frac{3}{4}$ $\frac{4}{4}$

$\frac{4}{4}$ = 4 beats per measure. The ♩ gets 1 beat.

$\frac{3}{4}$ = 3 beats per measure. The ♩ gets 1 beat.

31. trill *tr*

Quick alternation of the written note and the note a step above.

32. upbeat

Incomplete notes in the first measure. Also called pick-up note(s).

GOLD STAR CERTIFICATE

CONGRATULATIONS,
Gold Star Performer!

You have completed the Piano Adventures
Gold Star Performance, Level 2B.

Write your name in the star to celebrate your progress!